Learning to Program with RobotC®

Learning to Program with RobotC®

A Crash Course

Alex Crow

with Gregory Crow

Learning to Program with RobotC®
Copyright © 2013 by Alex Crow and Gregory Crow

Printed in the United States of America.
Design, editing, and production: Steve Lewis
Cover robot image © Kirsty Pargeter|Dreamstime.com, Used by permission.
LEGO® and MINDSTORMS® are trademarks of The LEGO Group which is not overseeing, involved with, or responsible for this product.
FIRST® and FIRST® Tech Challenge are registered trademarks of FIRST® (www.usfirst.org) which is not overseeing, involved with, or responsible for this product.
Tetrix® is a registered trademark of Pitsco, Inc.
RobotC® is a registered trademark of Robomatter, Inc.
Logitech® is a registered trademark of Logitech International SA.
K'NEX℠ is a registered service mark of K'NEX Limited Partnership Group.
ANSI℠ is a registered service mark of American National Standards Institute.

ISBN: 978-0-9892807-9-2
Library of Congress Control Number: 2013949321

 Published by Eagle Trail Press Box 3671 Parker, Colorado 80134
info@EagleTrailPress.com

Contents

Why We Wrote This Book

When I (Alex) first became interested in robotics, my Dad (Gregory) and I looked for a "toolkit" I could use to try out some of my ideas. We found that LEGO® MINDSTORMS® and the Tetrix® kits did exactly what I needed, and that RobotC® was the perfect way to create the "brains" for my projects.

When I started to learn RobotC® I was always looking for information on the programming language itself. What is a function? What is a variable? How can I make program statements that get the robot to do what I want it to do? I could find a lot of this information on the Internet, so I got good practice doing research, too.

The nice thing about RobotC® is that it has a really logical structure, and I was able to learn how to write useful programs fairly quickly. I got an appreciation for coding style, *and* I could see immediate results when I ran my programs. I could actually make the machines move and turn! It was a lot of fun.

As I began to use more sophisticated machine parts, like infrared or sonar sensors, my programs started getting more complicated. Like most students, I tend to jump in and just start "doing stuff." What I needed was a way to keep track of everything. I needed a better process for putting it all together and making sure everything worked the way it was supposed to work.

My Dad helped me learn about some of the real-life principles of software design that are used today by professional programmers, and we worked on getting hands-on practice. I learned how important it was to keep good documentation, and especially how to put meaningful comments inside my programs themselves.

On more than one project I was able to practice all of the principles of software design from beginning to end, and I found that it really helped me to be successful. I was able to design and create a real working robot from the parts we bought, and I wrote the programs to make that robot do all of the things it was required to do.

Afterward we decided to write a report that showed all the steps I had followed, with specific examples along the way. Once we finished, I thought this could actually help other kids get a quicker start on learning how to program and have fun with robotics.

We developed this book as an introduction to the whole process, so it is not really a detailed programming tutorial. There are other resources kids can use to learn about the features of RobotC®, for example. What we wanted to do was give kids a taste for how real programmers work, and how kids can use those same processes to do the things they want with their own robots. Anyone in sixth grade or higher should be able to use the ideas in this book.

We really hope that you enjoy this book, and that you find it helpful as you learn more about robotics and programming. The most important thing is to have more fun with robots!

Alex Crow

The Building Blocks

What is Robotics?

The word "robotics" can mean different things to different people, so let's start with a common definition.

Official Definition: "Robotics is the branch of technology that deals with the design, construction, operation, and application of robots, as well as computer systems for their control, sensory feedback, and information processing. These technologies deal with automated machines that can take the place of humans in dangerous environments or manufacturing processes, or resemble humans in appearance, behavior, and/or cognition."

That's a mouthful with a lot of big terms, so where do we begin? How about this?

Robotics is simply the making of robots.

The goal of this book is to help you understand some general concepts of robotics, and especially how to program robots to do the things you want them to do. We will also talk about the fundamentals of requirements and teamwork, because they are both important for building a working robot. Getting the job done requires several different kinds of skills, good working relationships with others, and a clear understanding of what to build.

Life Cycles

In the programming business, each piece of computer software is thought of as having a life of its own: from birth through retirement, and all the stages in between. It is important to plan for what happens in each of these stages, and that process is called managing the life cycle.

Official Definition: "Life Cycle Management is the process of managing the entire life of a product from its conception, through design and manufacturing, to service and disposal. It integrates people, data, processes, and business systems to provide a product information timeline for companies."

Hardware is the term that refers to the physical aspects of the robot, while *software* is the brains of the robot. Since a robot is a combination of hardware and software, there are at least two distinct life cycles that robot builders must consider. There is a third life cycle that involves the final product—in other words, what the eventual owner or user does with the completed robot. Each of these life cycles is important and need to be coordinated,

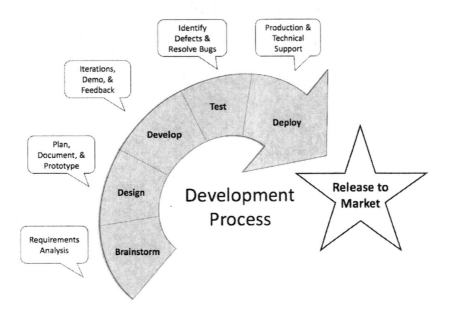

but we will be focusing only on the software life cycle in this book.

The chart above shows the stages in the Software Development Life Cycle (SDLC). As you can see, there are five major steps in this process. It is crucial that each step is completed prior to moving to the next step. We will talk about each of these steps in the sections below.

Requirements

The first step in the development process involves brainstorming and thinking about what you want the robot to be and to do. An important part of this stage is to write down your requirements for the robot.

Official Definition: "A requirement is a single documented physical or functional need that a particular product or process must be able to perform. It is a statement that identifies a necessary attribute, capability, characteristic, or quality that has value to someone, usually the product owner. The product owner or ultimate user is the person whose needs must be considered as the product is being developed."

The number of requirements will vary from product to product, but generally requirements analysis is completed when the end result is defined well enough so that a prototype or model can be constructed. Remember that requirements are not designs. There may be several designs that could meet the requirements, so requirements should not dictate the design.

A Sample of Poor Requirements

1. It should be square
2. It should go forward
3. It picks up things

These ideas are a start for telling the designer what to build, but they are not specific, they are incomplete, and they are vague. The examples below are a bit more detailed, but they should be specified even more. Just remember, the better the requirements, the better the outcome or product.

Better Example Requirements

1. It must be remote controlled by a user
2. It must be able to carry 2 lbs of payload over smooth terrain

3. It has to fit into an 18" x 15" x 9" box

4. It must be battery operated

The above examples start to outline what the product owner really wants to have built. It gives the designers enough information to get started. With more detailed requirements, the developers can better understand what they should be designing.

Something that would make these requirements even more meaningful are "Use Cases." These are a list of steps that specify interactions between a person and a product. They answer the questions: How is this used by someone? What does this do for the person?

A Use Case Example

Here is an example Use Case for one of the requirements we listed earlier: It must be able to be remote controlled by a user.

> Use Case: Jeremy is a user of the robot. He wants to control the robot wirelessly using his computer with an attached joystick. He wants to be able to turn the robot 360 degrees (spin it in a circle). He expects to use the remote control to drive forward, backward, and turn to the left and right, as well as to stop. Jeremy is planning to enter a contest where the robots will be required to have at minimum top speed of 8 miles per hour.

Good Use Cases should be as detailed as possible and should illustrate specific uses of the robot by giving real life examples. This helps the developers to specify exactly what they need to design.

Teamwork

In order to construct most projects, there are different resources and sets of skills that are needed by the team. The making of a robot can be broken down into many steps. In its simplest terms robots need hardware (construction of the physical parts) and software (programming logic). Depending on the requirements, even those two areas should be broken down into more detailed aspects. Hardware could be broken down into building the main assembly, the mechanical arm, drive train, etc. Software could involve programming the remote control, operating the mechanical arm, regulating speed and direction, etc.

Each of the team members must be working from the same requirements. Usually, all of the team members need to be involved from the beginning to fully understand what their tasks will be during the project. If one member does all the work, the others soon defer to them and typically innovation and productivity are smothered. If multiple people review the requirements and participate in building the Use Cases and the design, the project has a better chance of meeting the requirements.

Design

Now that we have reviewed requirements, the details behind requirements, and their critical importance, we can move ahead with the design.

Even though all of the features of a robot need to be designed, we are going to focus specifically on the design of the software or programming that will control the behavior of the robot.

Official Definition: "Software design is the process of implementing solutions to one or more sets of defined problems or requirements using programming."

There are several different concepts to understand in order to design software. The following list shows a few of these ideas:

Compatibility – The software must be able to work together with all of the other parts of the product, whether they are hardware or other pieces of software.

Extensibility – Design the software so it can be extended, so that new capabilities or functions can be added without changing the existing foundation.

Fault Tolerance – Make the software so it can resist and recover from failures.

Maintainability – Build the software so it is easy to maintain over the its lifetime.

Modularity – Construct the software from small pieces of code or components that each do one thing very well. This makes it easier for many people to work on the project, and it allows for easier testing and isolation of problems.

Reliability – Make sure the software continues to be reliable, working exactly the way it was designed over its lifetime.

Reusability – Build software components that can be plugged in and reused with little or no modification for accomplishing additional tasks in the program.

Robustness – The software should be built to take as much stress as required, based on the different conditions forced upon it over its lifetime.

Security – Make the software safe from being tampered with by unauthorized people.

Usability – Be sure the software is easy to use in various conditions, rather than being overly complicated.

Performance – The software should perform its functions perfectly in an acceptable amount of time.

Scalability - The software should be able to do its job for as many users or processes as it is required to serve.

Design Documents

As the design starts to take shape, most people will use a whiteboard or a similar method to collaborate and share their ideas, to explore different ways of meeting the requirements. Here is an example of how the design of a component starts to take shape on a whiteboard.

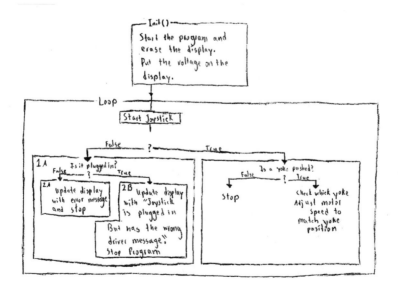

Once this level of understanding is reached, then a Software Design Document (SDD) is created to capture all of the details that should be included in the actual program. There are many different documentation methods for creating the SDD, and they vary based on organization and personal preference.

The SDD is required in order to coordinate the activities of a large team toward their ultimate deliverable, which is all the required software to run a fully functioning robot. The SDD needs to define all parts of the software and how they will work together. Most SSDs will have a High Level Design section (HLD) which looks at the project from a general perspective, maintaining a simplicity or overview based on the whiteboard discussions. The developers will usually create a Low Level Design section (LLD) which contains the little important details of exactly how each component will be built. This is useful for reviewing the project with all of the team members who are working on the individual components, ensuring that they will all work together correctly when assembled into the finished product.

Pseudo Code

Once the developers have started the process of designing the software, they may want to generate "pseudo code" to convey their ideas and concepts for how the software will eventually work.

Official Definition: "Pseudo code is a high level method of communicating structural conventions for human understanding vs. machine interpretation."

Pseudo code can vary from user to user, but typically it represents the program logic in a way that anyone should be able to follow. Below is a sample of a C function represented using pseudo code:

```
function fizzbuzz
    for (number between 1 to 100)
        set print_it to true;
        if number is divisible by 3
            print "Fizz";
            set print_it to false;
        if number is divisible by 5
            print "Buzz";
            set print_it to false;
        if print_it, print number;
        print a newline character;
```

Development

Software development is the process of writing computer code which will control the robot and allow it to do the tasks required of it. Just as there are many design approaches, there seem to be almost the same number of development approaches. Some of these are identified by names such as Procedural, Modular, Imperative, Object-Oriented, Functional, Logical, and Structured. The one we will be using is called "structured programming," since it can be applied using any computer language.

Official Definition: "Structured programming employs a top-down design model, in which developers map out the overall program structure into separate subsections.

Program logic follows a simple hierarchical model that uses looping (*for* and *while*), and groups similar functions into separate modules."

A computer programming language is an artificial language that is converted to machine instructions for the hardware during the compiling process. This allows the program logic to interact with the machine and to control its behavior. The language we will be using is called RobotC®. This is a derivative of the standard ANSI C language, and it is a great foundation for young developers to build upon.

Prototyping

In a typical software development process, most developers use a prototyping process. Prototyping allows the developer to get feedback on his program before he gets too far into the development cycle and finds out he is not designing the kind of product that the owner or user really wants. The developer will work through a set of basic requirements to create a unit of code, and then he will show that work to the product owner to get feedback and approval to continue programming. Based on the feedback he receives, the developer might change the design or approach to the project before continuing.

Here is an example that helps to illustrate how the prototyping process works. One developer has been assigned to create a piece of code that allows the user to turn the robot 90 degrees to the right. Assuming that the robot hardware was available for testing, the developer would load his code on the LEGO® NXT brick to test how the robot moves. If the robot only turned 80 degrees, then the developer would adjust the code and work with the robot builder to determine why it didn't function as planned and how to make it work better.

Start Using RobotC®

Here we will focus on a few samples of the RobotC® language. First, you must have downloaded and installed *RobotC® for LEGO® MINDSTORMS®*, and it is also helpful to load the additional component called *LEGO® MINDSTORMS® Virtual Worlds* for testing your code. To start a new program, follow these steps:

1. Change Menu Level to Expert using
   ```
   Window > Menu Level > Expert
   ```
2. Change Platform to FTC® using
   ```
   Robot > Platform Type > FIRST® Tech
   Challenge
   ```
3. Close RobotC® and Reopen
4. Open a blank file using
   ```
   File > New
   ```
   or Ctrl + N

Now there will be a blank form for you to start entering your first program. Don't forget to save your work often with Ctrl + S.

Learning the Language

The following sections show you different features or statements in the RobotC® programming language.

Comments

The most important part of programming may not be what you think it is. Most people think it involves writing logical instructions to perform tasks. However, the most important part of programming is writing clear comments in your code. It is very likely that the first time you write a program, that code will be revisited by you or another person to change, update, or improve it in the future. Inserting clear comments makes it much easier and faster to improve your code, because the comments make it clear what the purpose of the code was from the beginning.

There are two ways to add comments. The first is a single line method by putting two slash characters (//) in front of the comment text. The other is a block text method where the beginning of the comment starts with /* and ends with */. A RobotC® function built from the previous pseudo code example would definitely benefit from comments, as shown below.

```
/* This is a comment using a text block
   for the function fizzbuzz */
void function fizzbuzz {
   // Single line comment.
   // Start a loop from 1 to 100
   for (i = 1; i<=100; i++) {
      // True: the number will be printed
      set print_number = true;
```

Define Statements

If there is a constant that will be used over and over, many developers set that value with a #define statement. This gives the programmer the guarantee that the value will always be the same each time it is referenced in the program.

```
/* This #define statement sets the
variable IR_STRENGTH to a constant
value of 300 */
#define    IR_STRENGTH    300
```

Variables

A *variable* is a named storage location that contains some type of information known as a *value*. Variables allow the programmer to reference information throughout the program while having the option of changing the values based on different inputs during the program's run cycle. In RobotC®, lines defining variables always end with a semicolon.

```
// Set two integer variables to the value
// of zero. Integers hold whole numbers.
int irDirection, irStrength = 0;
// Set motor power to a value of 30.
int motorPower = 30;
// Set a string variable to the value of
// "right." Strings hold text.
string leftorright = "right";
```

Functions

Functions contain sets of programming instructions used to perform a specific task. In other programming languages, functions may be called subroutines. Functions can be coded within the program flow, or they can be stored in a separate library or header file and called when needed. Developers may want to put functions in a separate library if they are planning to use those capabilities in several different programs. The individual programs can call the functions from the same library, and the programmer only has one place to look for them or maintain them.

Functions have three requirements:

- function name
- start with an open curly brace {
- end with a close curly brace }

In RobotC®, any function that is not the *main* function, must be typed above the actual main function (*main* is discussed later in pages below). The following are some examples of the built-in functions for the brick display that are available to be used with RobotC® and LEGO® MINDSTORMS®:

```
// Write debug to the brick display.
writeDebugStreamLine("text");
// Write the text LPM=15 on line 3.
nxtDisplayTextLine(3, "LPM=%d", 15);
// Erase the brick display.
eraseDisplay();
// Stop processing in the program for a
// specific amount of time.
// 1000 milliseconds = one second.
wait1Msec (1000);
```

Header Files

As noted earlier, header files contain reusable code that can be called by or included in any program. They are easy to reference and can be used whenever the functions are needed by the external programs. Special functions, called *drivers*, are typically used whenever a particular hardware device needs to be controlled by a program. Drivers will be either in the form of a library or header file.

```
// This statement includes the driver
// functions for a particular device.
#include "drivers/irseeker-v2.h"
```

Main

Every program in RobotC® must have what is called a *main* function. When the program begins to run it will look for the main function and execute the statements in a top to bottom sequence. If the program comes to a different named function, it will execute the instructions in that function before returning where it left off in the main routine. Here is an example of the flow of a program with a main function.

```
/*** FUNCTION LIST ***/
// Update the brick display.
void updateDisplay()
{
    // Erase display.
    eraseDisplay();
    // Write some debug to the brick
    writeDebugStreamLine("Dis=%d",
SensorValue[sonarSensor]);
    writeDebugStreamLine("LSvalue=%d",
SensorValue(lightSensor));
```

```
}
// Main function
task main()
{    // Beginning of the main function.
     // Wait for a one second.
     wait1Msec (1000);
     // Update the display.
     updateDisplay();
}    // End of the main function.
```

This program starts at the main function, then it waits for one second, and finally it updates the display with some sensor values before exiting.

Pragma Statements

A pragma, or directive, is a language construct that specifies how a compiler should process the input in the program. Pragma statements are not part of the programming language, and they usually vary from compiler to compiler. In this crash course, we are using the LEGO® MINDSTORMS® interactive compiler, so we need to use the following formats. MINDSTORMS® allows the programmer to easily select and change the pragma statements based on their sensors and motors.

```
// IR Seeker on port 2 of brick.
#pragma config(Sensor, S2, IRSeeker,
sensorI2CCustom)
// Sonar sensor on port 3.
#pragma config(Sensor, S3, sonarSensor,
sensorSONAR)
```

```
// Light Sensor on port 4.
#pragma config(Sensor, S4, lightSensor,
sensorLightActive)
```

Please see the code samples below for other example programs to try on your own.

Quality Testing

Quality testing, sometimes called Quality Assurance or QA for short, involves testing the software to be sure it reliably does what it is supposed to do.

Official Definition: "Quality Assurance consists of the activities that are implemented to review, test, and possibly correct any program code which does not meet the requirements for a deliverable." It involves comparing the behavior of the software against either the original requirements or the requirements as they were modified during the prototyping stage.

QA ensures that the software meets or exceeds the requirements for the product. In some cases, QA may actually be performed before the deliverable is completed to support the programmer during the initial testing phases. The QA process has a formal test plan and specific Use Cases for completing each test satisfactorily.

Deployment

Deployment is the final phase during which the product or deliverable is accepted and used by the product owner. It involves using the completed software in the finished robot.

Using SDLC Concepts

What follows is an example software development project that puts all the pieces together for you, using Software Development Life Cycle concepts to create a functioning product.

The Challenge

This chapter is adapted from my (Alex) programming project for the 2013 FIRST® FTC® "RING IT UP℠" contest which had two challenges. A robot was to be built that could collect and hang rings on hooks at several heights. There would be a thirty second autonomous course where the robot must hang rings all by itself. The final part of this challenge was a two minute driver-controlled course where one or two operators helped the robot to hang as many rings as possible.

Requirements

The first step in the Software Development Life Cycle is to gather the requirements for the project.

Use Case #1

In the Autonomous Period, robots run by them-selves for thirty seconds. Infrared beacons are placed randomly on a peg in the tic-tac-toe board prior to the start of the match. Each robot can begin with one specially-marked autonomous ring. Rings that are not scored are removed by referees after the Autonomous Period ends. Several sensors are available to help the robot locate the IR beacon, including light/dark sensors, infrared sensors, and several others.

Requirements

1. The light sensor must be mounted no higher than 1 cm from the ground to function correctly.
2. The operation must be completed autonomously within 30 seconds.
3. Once the plastic ring is hung on the rack, the robot must lower the manipulator arm in order to have the ring count as being hung on the rack.
4. There is a program that teams download which separates the autonomous code from the driver controlled code.
5. There is a white stripe of tape on the black floor which leads to the peg that the ring will hang on.

Assumptions

1. The IR beacon signal will be strong enough to reach the robot at the starting point.
2. The robot must be 20 cm from the base of the hanging poles in order to raise the manipulator arm in front of the lip of the pole.
3. The robot must advance 5 cm once the manipulator arm is raised in order to let the plastic ring hang on the pole.

Use Case #2

During the two minute Driver-Controlled Period, teams can use standard game pad controllers, each with two joysticks to operate their robots. For this sample program we decided to use a Logitech® F310 Gamepad.

Requirements

1. Two team members can control the robot at the same time.
2. One team will partner with another team for each match.
3. There is a 1/2" board next to the peg that the robot must accelerate to in order to get over the top.
4. The drivers only have two minutes to hang as many rings as possible.
5. Thirty seconds before the driver controlled portion ends, team members are allowed to lift each other for bonus points.
6. Only two rings can be held at a time.

7. Rings dropped on the center board are one point each for the team that left it, and those rings cannot be moved off the board.

8. Opponents cannot ram into each other.

Assumptions

1. You can start anywhere you want as long as your robot is touching the wall.

2. The robot will have enough power to get on top of the board.

Design

The graphic below shows the playing field. In it you can see the IR Beacon line leading to the pegs from the corner. The corner rack is not depicted in the image. If your robot is able to detect heavy rings, then you can hang the heavy rings on that corner rack.

Courtesy of www.usfirst.org

Here are some of the design features we selected for this challenge. The robot will have four motors: two in the front and two in the back. They will each be geared with big-to-little gears. This gives the robot the ability to drive faster than normal, and that will be useful for driving over the half-inch board. To hang the ring we will use a drawer slider mechanism moved by a motor. The actual ring holder will be doubled and have bars to hold the rings in place. This will enable the robot to hang two rings at once.

During the autonomous challenge, the robot will have an IR Seeker placed next to the ring holder to search for the correct peg. The robot will have two ultrasonic sensors in the front to look out for passing robots as it is searching for the peg. Finally, a color sensor will be used to distinguish white from black to find, follow, and adjust to the white line on the black board. All the design options described in this paragraph can be changed as needed to create the best design for accomplishing the challenge.

Hardware Design Sketches

Robot Top View

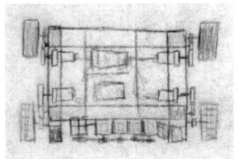

In this sketch the placement of motors and the positions of the gears can be seen. The battery and brick are also shown. Note that the omni-wheels are on the front of the robot.

Robot Front View

In this sketch the placement of the ultrasonic sensors and IR Seeker are shown. This view shows the chain mechanism that will raise the arm and the ring holder design. Also there is a resistor that will be used to reduce the slack in the chain.

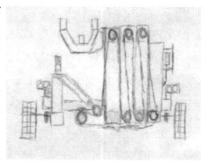

Robot Side View

In this sketch the placement of the motors and gears are emphasized. The wheels are drawn to be "see-through" so that the inner workings could be shown. Also there is a shield to protect the battery and brick.

Joystick Top View

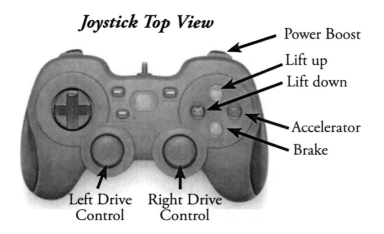

Power Boost

Lift up

Lift down

Accelerator

Brake

Left Drive Control

Right Drive Control

Software Designs

Two programs must be created, one for each of the challenges.

1. The autonomous program
2. The joystick program

These could be combined into a single program, but for this example they will be two separate programs.

Pseudo Code

Here are some examples of pseudo code that represent functions needed during each part of the challenge.

Autonomous Mode

This example pseudo code is based on the known conditions and the assumptions given in the requirements.

```
While (Running) // Endless loop
If I can see the IR beacon,
    • Follow it until exactly 28 cm from the
      wall the IR Beacon is attached to.
If wall is found,
    • Stop the robot.
    • Adjust   position   to   get   correct
      distance.
Else // I can't see the IR Beacon
    • End program as we cannot see the IR
      Beacon and cannot continue.
```

Joystick Operation

- Create a Deadzone and Max joystick-to-motor value

While (Running) // Endless loop
- Run the motors at the value of the joystick

Development

This development code is shown only for illustration, and it does not represent the complete program. For example, the routines for hanging the rings on the pegs are not included.

Joystick Operation Sample Program

This program allows a joystick to control the robot.

```
#pragma config(Hubs, S1, HTMotor, none,
  none, none)
#pragma config(Motor, mtr_S1_C1_1,
  leftMotor, tmotorTetrix, openLoop,
  reversed)
#pragma config(Motor, mtr_S1_C1_2,
  rightMotor, tmotorTetrix, openLoop)
//*!!Code automatically generated by
  'ROBOTC' configuration wizard !!*//
// The motors are assigned by ports.
// leftMotor is plugged into S1 port of
// Controller 1 (C1) and powered by slot 1
// The following pragma statement would
// be added for a servo in S2 port of
```

```
// Controller 1 (C1) on slot 6.
// #pragma config(Servo, srvo_S2_C1_6,
// release, tServoStandard)

// This includes the library to make the
// joystick work.
#include "JoystickDriver.c"

// Set this to true so when starting the
// program, it runs forever in a loop.
bool RUNNING = true;

// **********************************
//              FUNCTIONS
// **********************************
// This function allows the program to
// look for a deadzone and max joystick
// to motor value.
int scaleForMotor(int joyValue)
{
  // If the joystick is pushed less than
  // +5 or -5, it's basically idle, set
  // power to zero. This could be a
  // #define above, but this works too.
  const int DEADZONE = 5;

  // Check for deadzone using the abs
  // function to get the absolute value
  // and test if we are in the deadzone
  // for the joystick.
```

```
if(abs(joyValue) < DEADZONE)
{
  // Return a zero so the program sends
  // 0% power to the motors.
  return 0;
}


// The joystick goes between -127 and
// +127, but motors only go to -100 and
// +100. Check if the joystick value is
// greater than 100, then return 100.
if(joyValue > 100)
{
  //The motors cannot go over 100 so
  // just return 100%.
  return 100;
}
 // If the joystick value is less than
 // -100, return -100.
else if(joyValue < -100)
{
  return -100;
}
//Otherwise, return the value of the
// joystick.
else
{
  return joyValue;
}
} // End of function
```

```
// Main task of the program
task main()
{
  // Call out the function enabling the
  // joystick to control the robot and get
  // the values of buttons/controls.
  getJoystickSettings(joystick);

  // While the robot is running.
  while(RUNNING)
  {
   // Display the Battery levels.
   // This line prints out the label on
   // line 1 (0 identifies line 1 of display
   // 1 identifies display line 2, etc.)
   nxtDisplayTextLine(0, "Battery
Levels");
   // This line prints out the average
   // value of the internal battery on
   // line 2 of the display.
   nxtDisplayTextLine(1, "int-Avg %3.1fV",
nAvgBatteryLevel / (float) 1000);
   // This line prints out the immediate
   // value of the internal battery on
   // line 3 of the display.
   nxtDisplayTextLine(2, "int-Now %3.1fV",
nImmediateBatteryLevel / (float) 1000);
   // This line prints out the average
   // value of the external battery on
   // line 4 of the display.
```

```
nxtDisplayTextLine(3, "ext-Avg %3.1fV",
externalBatteryAvg / (float) 1000);
  // This line prints out the immediate
  // value of the external battery on
  // line 5 of the display.
nxtDisplayTextLine(4, "ext-Now %3.1fV",
externalBattery / (float) 1000);


  // This refreshes the joystick values
  // from the controller.
  getJoystickSettings(joystick);


  // Run the left motor as described in
  // the scale for motor function. This
  // is the left joystick yoke.
  motor[mtr_S1_C1_1] =
scaleForMotor(joystick.joy1_y1);
  // Run the right motor also described
  // in the scale for motor function. This
  // is the right joystick yoke.
  motor[mtr_S1_C1_2] =
scaleForMotor(joystick.joy1_y2);


  // This code would be used for the
  // buttons desired for a servo. Sample
  // only, and commented out as there are
  // no servos currently on the robot.
  // Check for button 9 being pushed on
  // the joystick.
```

```
//if(joy1Btn(9))
//{
//   servo[release]=360;
//}
// Check for stop being pushed.
// (button 10).
//else if(joy1Btn(10))
//{
//   servo[release] = 0;
//}


} // End of while loop.


} // End of main task.
```

Autonomous Operation Sample Program

This program is a simple autonomous operation program allowing the robot to follow an IR Signal until it reaches 28 centimeters from a wall or object.

```
#pragma config(Hubs, S1, HTMotor, none,
none, none)
#pragma config(Sensor, S2, sonarSensor,
sensorSONAR)
#pragma config(Sensor, S3, IRSeeker, sen-
sorI2CCustom)
#pragma config(Motor, mtr_S1_C1_1, leftMo-
tor, tmotorTetrix, openLoop, reversed)
#pragma config(Motor, mtr_S1_C1_2, rightMo-
tor, tmotorTetrix, openLoop)
```

```
//*!! Code automatically generated by
'ROBOTC' configuration wizard !!*//


// Includes drivers for the IRSeeker.
#include "drivers/hitechnic-irseeker-v2.h"


// *********************************
// Global Constants
// Minimum of -100 and maximum of +100 for
// motors.
#define BOUND(n) (((n) < -100)? -100: ((n)
> 100)? 100: (n))
// Will need to test for how close we are
// to the beacon.
#define IR_STRENGTH  300
// Set factorPower default.
int factorPower = 1;
// Set how much to scale up the
// factorPower for speed.
int scalingPower = 11;
// Set initial values for variables that
// store readings coming from the beacon.
// 1-4 is on the left
// 1 is solely the acS0
// 2 is acS0 and acS1
// 3 is solely the acS1
// 4 is acS1 and acS2
// 5 is straight ahead
// 5 is solely acS2
```

```
// 6-9 is on the right
// 6 is acS2 and acS3
// 7 is solely acS3
// 8 is acS3 and acS4
// 9 is solely acS4
int acS0 = 0, acS1 = 0, acS2 = 0,
acS3 = 0, acS4 = 0;
// Initialize the direction and strength
// variables to zero.
int irDirection, irStrength = 0;
// Set motor power to 35%.
int motorPower = 35;
// Set the distance that we want in cm
// from the peg pole.
int distance_in_cm = 28;
// Set which direction we will go,
// left or right.
string leftorright = "right";


// ***********************************
//                 Functions
// ***********************************
// This updates the display with the
// latest information.
void updateDisplay()
{
  // Erase the display.
  eraseDisplay();
  // Update the text on the display
  // for direction and strength.
```

```
    nxtDisplayTextLine(1, "D=%d / S=%d",
irDirection, irStrength);
    writeDebugStreamLine("D=%d / S=%d",
irDirection, irStrength);
    nxtDisplayTextLine(2, "S1=%d / S3=%d",
acS1, acS3);
    nxtDisplayTextLine(3, "LPM=%d", motor-
Power);
    nxtDisplayTextLine(4, "RPM=%d", motor-
Power);
    writeDebugStreamLine("S1=%d / S3=%d",
acS1, acS3);
    writeDebugStreamLine("LPM=%d", motor-
Power);
    writeDebugStreamLine("RPM=%d", motor-
Power);
    nxtDisplayTextLine(5, "intbat %3.1fV",
nImmediateBatteryLevel / (float) 1000);
    nxtDisplayTextLine(6, "extbat %3.1fV",
externalBattery / (float) 1000);
    writeDebugStreamLine("Dis=%d",
SensorValue[sonarSensor]);
}


// **********************************
// This function reads the value of the
// IR sensor detectors, direction, and
// summary signal strength.
bool getBeaconSignal()
{
```

```
// Write debug to the brick display.
// Erase the display each time.
eraseDisplay();
// These lines will let us know that
// we are in this function.
nxtDisplayTextLine(7, "In getBeaconSig-
nal");
writeDebugStreamLine("In getBeaconSig-
nal");


// See if the individual signal
// strengths of the internal sensors
// can be read. The ! means "not."
if (!HTIRS2readAllACStrength(IRSeeker,
acS0, acS1, acS2, acS3, acS4))
  {
    // If we can't read the values, we
    // error out as our IR Sensor is dead.
    return false;
  }
// See if the enhanced direction and
// strength are set. The ! means
// "not."
if (!HTIRS2readEnhanced(IRSeeker, irDi-
rection, irStrength))
  {
    // If we can't read the values, we
    // error out as our IR Sensor is dead.
    return false;
  }
```

```
  // Update the display with the values.
  updateDisplay();

  return true;
}  // End of getBeaconSignal function.


// ***********************************
// This function drives toward the IR
// beacon and squares up until it finds
// the wall or another object.
bool driveTowardBeacon()
{
  // Write debug to the brick display.
  eraseDisplay();
  // These lines display on the brick
  // and let us know what function we are
  // currently in.
  nxtDisplayTextLine(7, "In driveToward-
Beacon");
  writeDebugStreamLine("In driveTowardBea-
con");

  // Now read the internal sensors values.
  getBeaconSignal();

  // While the IR signals are less than
  // IR_STRENGTH, go through this loop.
  while (irStrength < IR_STRENGTH)
  {
```

```
// Read the individual signal
// strengths of the internal
// sensor detectors.
getBeaconSignal();

// If sonar sensor doesn't see a wall or
// object yet, use the IR beacon.
if (SensorValue(sonarSensor) >= dis-
tance_in_cm)
  {
    // First check to see if IR direction
    // is 5, then just go straight ahead.
    if (irDirection == 5)
    {
      // Set both motors to the same power
      // Left motor.
      motor[mtr_S1_C1_1] = motorPower+5;
      // Right motor.
      motor[mtr_S1_C1_2] = motorPower+5;
      //Update the display.
      updateDisplay();
      nxtDisplayTextLine(3, "LPM=%d",
motorPower + 5);
      nxtDisplayTextLine(4, "RPM=%d",
motorPower + 5);
      writeDebugStreamLine("LPM=%d",
motorPower + 5);
      writeDebugStreamLine("RPM=%d",
motorPower + 5);
    }
```

```
      // If the beacon is not directly in
      // front of us.
      else
      {
        // We are off-course, so adjust.
        // example: (30 * 1)*.5
        // factorPower formula is
        // (senszoneforstraight minus
        // currentdirection) times
        // factorforscalingforpower
        factorPower = ((5 - irDirection) *
scalingPower);
        // This needs to be between 0 - 100
        // so we need some min/max checking.
        // Adjust right motor so we have a
        // motor power between 0 and 100.
        motor[mtr_S1_C1_2] =
BOUND(motorPower + factorPower);
        // Adjust left motor too.
        motor[mtr_S1_C1_1] =
BOUND(motorPower - factorPower);


        // Write debug to display the motor
        // settings.
        updateDisplay();
        nxtDisplayTextLine(3, "LPM=%d",
BOUND(motorPower - factorPower) );
        nxtDisplayTextLine(4, "RPM=%d",
BOUND(motorPower + factorPower) );
```

```
     writeDebugStreamLine("BOUNDLPM=%d",
BOUND(motorPower - factorPower));
     writeDebugStreamLine("BOUNDRPM=%d",
BOUND(motorPower + factorPower));
  }
  // Let it move and reevaluate in 100
  // milliseconds (1/10th of a second).
  wait1Msec (100);

  // Check to see if we are going to hit
  // a pole or object.
  if(SensorValue(sonarSensor) <=
distance_in_cm)
    {
    // Too close; back up for half a
    // second and look for signal
    // again.
    // Stop moving.
    motor[mtr_S1_C1_1] = 0;
    motor[mtr_S1_C1_2] = 0;
    wait1Msec(1000);

    // Back up.
    motor[mtr_S1_C1_1] = -20;
    motor[mtr_S1_C1_2] = -20;
    wait1Msec(500);

    // Stop moving.
    motor[mtr_S1_C1_1] = 0;
    motor[mtr_S1_C1_2] = 0;
```

```
      wait1Msec(1000);
      break;
   }
   // Check the value of the left and
   // right IR detector to go left or
   // right.
   else if (((acS1 > 15 ) || (irStrength
<= 70)) && (time1[T1] >= 3000))
      {
         // The beacon is on the robot's
         // left, so we should spin left to
         // see the wall or object.
         // Set direction.
         leftorright = "left";

         writeDebugStreamLine("In acs1 timer
check");
         // If we are less than 28cm away
         // then break out of the loop.
         if (SensorValue(sonarSensor) <=
distance_in_cm)
         {
            break;
         }
      }
   // Check the value of the left and
   // right IR detector to go left or
   // right.
   else if (((acS3 > 15) || (irStrength
<= 70)) && (time1[T1] >= 3000))
```

```
  {
    // Beacon is on robot's right, spin
    // right to see wall or object.
    leftorright = "right";

    writeDebugStreamLine("In acs3 timer
check");
    // If we are less than 28cm away
    // then break from loop.
    if (SensorValue(sonarSensor) <=
distance_in_cm)
      {
        break;
      }
    }
  }
  // We are done so return to main with
  // true.
  return true;
}


// *********************************
// Make sure we are exactly how far we
// need to be in case we overshot our
// goal of 28cm.
void getCorrectDistance()
{
  // Erase display.
  eraseDisplay();
```

```
// Write text on line 8 of display.
// "In getCorrectDistance"
nxtDisplayTextLine(7, "In getCorrectDis-
tance");

// We are very close to the pole, so
// back up now.
while(SensorValue[sonarSensor] <=
distance_in_cm)
  {
    // Right motor at -35% power
    motor[mtr_S1_C1_1] = -motorPower;
    // Left motor at -35% power
    motor[mtr_S1_C1_2] = -motorPower;
    // Display the values of
    // the motors.
    nxtDisplayTextLine(3, "LPM=%d",
(-motorPower));
    nxtDisplayTextLine(4, "RPM=%d",
(-motorPower));
  }
}


// ***********************************
task main()
{
  // Clear the timer before we start.
  ClearTimer(T1);
  // Check the signals to see if we can
  // see the beacon at all.
```

```
if (getBeaconSignal())
{
  // We have data, so proceed.
  // Drive toward the beacon signal.
  driveTowardBeacon();

  // Now test the distance.
  // May need to back up.
  getCorrectDistance();
}
// Else if we don't have signal.
else
{
  // Erase the display.
  eraseDisplay();
  // Display in big letters on line 2
  // "No IR"
  nxtDisplayCenteredBigTextLine (1,
"NO IR");
  // Display in big letters on line 3
  // "Signal"
   nxtDisplayCenteredBigTextLine (2,
"Signal");
  }
  // Jump for joy and end program.
}
```

Quality Testing

Quality assurance and acceptance testing were done to ensure that each of the components fulfilled the requirements in the Use Cases.

Actual Robot Hardware

The following are photos of the actual robot hardware that was built from the requirements and designs for this challenge. Although the manipulator arm was not yet constructed, the foundation is shown.

Hardware required to complete these tasks:

- Laptop or desktop computer with Bluetooth or WIFI capability
- LEGO® NXT Brick
- Tetrix® robot kit for rails, wheels, motors, wires, external battery, etc.
- IR Seeker, Sonar Sensor, and IR Beacon

Front View

Sonar Sensor   IR Sensor   Brick

Top View

DC Controller   Battery Pack

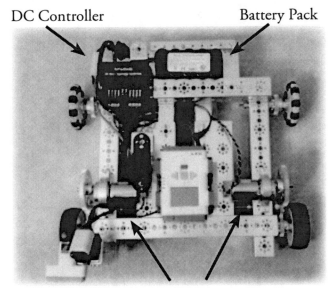

Motors

Side View

Rear omni-wheels for turning   Motor gears to drive the wheels   Front regular wheels for traction

Code Examples

The following are sample RobotC® programs that have been created and tested with *LEGO® MINDSTORMS® RobotC®* and *Virtual Worlds*. Feel free to enter them and test them, modifying them to learn how to make them do different things, too. Have fun!

Driving and Turning

```
// Drive forward for 1/2 second and stop.
// Turn right for 1/2 second and stop.
// Drive backward for 1/2 second, then stop.
#pragma config(Hubs, S1, HTMotor, HTMotor,
none, none)
#pragma config(Motor, mtr_S1_C1_1,
rightMotor, tmotorTetrix, openLoop)
#pragma config(Motor, mtr_S1_C1_2,
leftMotor, tmotorTetrix, openLoop, reversed)
```

```
//*!!Code automatically generated by 'ROBOTC'
configuration wizard !!*//

task main()
{
  // Valid entries for speed are between
  // -100 to +100 (percent power).
  // Right motor forward.
  motor[mtr_S1_C1_1] = 50;
  // Left motor forward.
  motor[mtr_S1_C1_2] = 50;

  // Now wait for 500 milliseconds.
  wait1Msec( 500 );

  // Right motor stop.
  motor[mtr_S1_C1_1] = 0;
  // Left motor stop.
  motor[mtr_S1_C1_2] = 0;

  // Turn right.
  // Right motor back.
  motor[mtr_S1_C1_1] = -50;
  // Left motor forward.
  motor[mtr_S1_C1_2] = 50;

  // Now wait for 500 milliseconds.
  wait1Msec( 500 );
```

```
// Right motor stop.
motor[mtr_S1_C1_1] = 0;
// Left motor stop
motor[mtr_S1_C1_2] = 0;


// Right motor back.
motor[mtr_S1_C1_1] = -50;
// Left motor back.
motor[mtr_S1_C1_2] = -50;


// Wait for 500 milliseconds (1/2 second)
wait1Msec( 500 );


// Right motor stop.
motor[mtr_S1_C1_1] = 0;
// Left motor stop.
motor[mtr_S1_C1_2] = 0;
} // End of program
```

Drive Until Reaching an Obstacle

```
// Drive forward with ultrasonic sensor until
// robot is 20 cm from a wall and then stop.
#pragma config(Sensor, S3, sonarSensor,
sensorSONAR)
#pragma config(Motor, mtr_S1_C1_1,
rightMotor, tmotorTetrix, openLoop)
#pragma config(Motor, mtr_S1_C1_2,
leftMotor, tmotorTetrix, openLoop, reversed)

//*!! Code automatically generated by
'ROBOTC' configuration wizard  !!*//

// ****************************************
// Includes
#include "drivers/hitechnic-irseeker-v2.h"

// Distance that we want to be from the wall
int distance_in_cm = 20;

task main()
{
  // Start driving ahead.
  // Right motor forward.
  motor[mtr_S1_C1_1] = 20;
  // Left motor forward.
  motor[mtr_S1_C1_2] = 20;
```

```
// Start an endless loop until the
// condition is no longer true.
// Quit when distance is less than 20cm.
while(SensorValue(sonarSensor) >=
      distance_in_cm)
{
  // Start moving ahead.
  // Right motor forward.
  motor[mtr_S1_C1_1] = 20;
  // Left motor forward.
  motor[mtr_S1_C1_2] = 20;
}

// This code will run after the while loop
// exits because the sensor shows distance
// of less than 20 cm.
// Right motor stop.
motor[mtr_S1_C1_1] = 0;
// Left motor stop.
motor[mtr_S1_C1_2] = 0;

} // End of program
```

Turning to Avoid Obstacles

```
// ****************************************
// This program moves robot forward until it
// sees an obstacle within 40cm and then it
// will turn left until it finds a clear area
// to continue driving.
// ****************************************
#pragma config(Hubs, S1, HTMotor, none, none,
none)
#pragma config(Sensor, S2, sonarSensor,
sensorSONAR)
#pragma config(Motor, mtr_S1_C1_1, leftMotor,
tmotorTetrix, openLoop, reversed)
#pragma config(Motor, mtr_S1_C1_2, rightMotor,
tmotorTetrix, openLoop)
//*!!Code automatically generated by 'ROBOTC'
configuration wizard  !!*//


// ****************************************
// Global Constants.
// Set the motor power.
int motorPower = 20;
// Set distance for locating obstacles.
int distance_in_cm = 40;
// Set boolean to be true and run forever.
bool RUNNING = true;
```

```
// Main task of the program
task main()
{
  // While the robot is running.
  while(RUNNING)
  {
    // Move forward if there is nothing
    // within 40cm.
    if(SensorValue[sonarSensor] >
distance_in_cm)
    {
      // Move forward at 20% power.
      // Left motor.
      motor[mtr_S1_C1_1] = motorPower;
      // Right motor.
      motor[mtr_S1_C1_2] = motorPower;
    }
    // But if there is something within 40cm
    else
    {
      // Turn left until there are no
      // obstacles in front of the robot
      // for 40cm.
      motor[mtr_S1_C1_1] = -motorPower;
      motor[mtr_S1_C1_2] = motorPower;
    }
  } // End of while loop running forever.

} // End of program.
```

Using Two Sensors to Avoid Obstacles

```
// ****************************************
// This program moves the robot forward until
// it sees an obstacle in front of it within
// 30cm and then it will turn left until it
// finds a clear area to drive in. It uses two
// sensors to allow the robot to see more of
// the surroundings and be more agile.
// ****************************************
#pragma config(Hubs, S1, HTMotor, none, none,
none)
#pragma config(Sensor, S2, sonarSensor,
sensorSONAR)
#pragma config(Sensor, S4, sonarSensor2,
sensorSONAR)
#pragma config(Motor, mtr_S1_C1_1, leftMotor,
tmotorTetrix, openLoop, reversed)
#pragma config(Motor,  mtr_S1_C1_2,
rightMotor, tmotorTetrix, openLoop)
//*!!Code automatically generated by 'ROBOTC'
configuration wizard  !!*//

//****************************************
// Global Constants.
// Set the motor power.
int motorPower = 20;
// Set distance for locating obstacles.
int distance_in_cm = 30;
```

```
// Set boolean to be true and run forever.
bool RUNNING = true;

// Main task of the program.
task main()
{
  // While the robot is running.
  while(RUNNING)
  {
    // Check if there is anything in the way
    // of either sensor.
    if((SensorValue[sonarSensor] >
distance_in_cm) && (SensorValue[sonarSensor2]
> distance_in_cm))
    {
      // Move forward at 20% power.
      motor[mtr_S1_C1_1] = motorPower;
      motor[mtr_S1_C1_2] = motorPower;
    }
    // But if there is something within 30cm.
    else
    {
      // Turn left until there are no
      // obstacles in front of the robot
      // for 30cm.
      motor[mtr_S1_C1_1] = -motorPower;
      motor[mtr_S1_C1_2] = motorPower;
    }
  } // End of the while running forever
} // End of program
```